W9-CNN-779

FAVORITE
BrandName
RECIPES™

easy pasta

pil

Publications International, Ltd.

Pictured on the front cover: Penne with Broccoli and Sausage *(page 88)*.

Pictured on the back cover *(top to bottom):* Reuben Noodle Bake *(page 24)*, Lentil and Orzo Pasta Salad *(page 34)* and Pesto Tortellini Soup *(page 64)*.

ISBN: 978-1-68022-013-1

Library of Congress Control Number: 2015934777

Manufactured in China.

8 7 6 5 4 3 2 1

Microwave Cooking: Microwave ovens vary in wattage. Use the cooking times as guidelines and check for doneness before adding more time.

Preparation/Cooking Times: Preparation times are based on the approximate amount of time required to assemble the recipe before cooking, baking, chilling or serving. These times include preparation steps such as measuring, chopping and mixing. The fact that some preparations and cooking can be done simultaneously is taken into account. Preparation of optional ingredients and serving suggestions is not included.

Publications International, Ltd.

contents

quick & cheesy

Southwestern Mac and Cheese

 1 package (8 ounces) uncooked elbow macaroni
 1 can (about 14 ounces) diced tomatoes with green peppers and
    onions
 1 can (10 ounces) diced tomatoes with mild green chiles
 1½ cups salsa
 3 cups (12 ounces) shredded Mexican cheese blend, divided

Slow Cooker Directions

1. Spray insert of slow cooker with nonstick cooking spray. Combine macaroni, tomatoes with juice, salsa and 2 cups cheese in slow cooker; mix well. Cover; cook on LOW 3 hours 45 minutes or until macaroni is tender.

2. Sprinkle remaining 1 cup cheese over macaroni. Cover; cook 15 minutes or until cheese is melted.

Makes 6 servings

Macaroni-Stuffed Peppers

3	green bell peppers, halved lengthwise and cored
1	cup uncooked elbow macaroni
2	tablespoons butter
½	cup finely chopped red bell pepper
2	tablespoons all-purpose flour
½	teaspoon salt
½	teaspoon paprika
¼	teaspoon black pepper
2	cups warm milk
1¾	cups (7 ounces) shredded sharp Cheddar cheese, divided
¼	cup panko bread crumbs

1. Preheat oven to 350°F. Spray 13×9-inch baking dish with nonstick cooking spray.

2. Bring large saucepan of water to a boil. Add pepper halves. Press with wooden spoon to submerge; boil 2 minutes. Remove peppers; drain well. Return water to a boil. Add macaroni; cook about 7 minutes or until al dente. Drain and return to saucepan.

3. Melt butter in large saucepan over medium heat. Add red bell pepper; cook and stir 5 minutes. Whisk in flour, salt, paprika and black pepper until smooth. Gradually whisk in milk until slightly thickened. Gradually stir in 1½ cups Cheddar cheese until melted and smooth. Stir in macaroni.

4. Arrange pepper halves cut sides up in prepared baking dish. Spoon macaroni mixture evenly into each pepper half. Combine remaining ¼ cup cheese and bread crumbs in small bowl. Sprinkle over macaroni.

5. Bake 20 to 25 minutes or until lightly browned and peppers are tender.

Makes 6 servings

Creamy Chicken and Pasta with Spinach

6	ounces uncooked egg noodles
2	boneless skinless chicken breasts (¾ pound), cooked and cut into 1-inch pieces
1	package (10 ounces) frozen chopped spinach, thawed and drained
1	can (4 ounces) sliced mushrooms, drained
1	tablespoon olive oil
¼	cup chopped onion
¼	cup chopped red bell pepper
2	cups (8 ounces) shredded Swiss cheese
1	container (8 ounces) sour cream
¾	cup half-and-half
2	eggs, lightly beaten
½	teaspoon salt

1. Preheat oven to 350°F. Spray 13×9-inch baking dish with nonstick cooking spray. Cook noodles according to package directions until al dente. Drain and place in large bowl. Add chicken, spinach and mushrooms; mix well.

2. Heat oil in large skillet over medium-high heat. Add onion and bell pepper; cook and stir 2 minutes or until onion is tender. Add to chicken mixture.

3. Combine Swiss cheese, sour cream, half-and-half, eggs and salt in medium bowl; mix well. Add to chicken mixture; stir until blended. Spoon into prepared baking dish.

4. Cover and bake 30 to 35 minutes or until heated through.

Makes 8 servings

Note: To cook chicken, place in saucepan or deep skillet; season with salt and add cold water to cover by 2 inches. Cover and bring to a simmer over medium-high heat. Reduce heat to medium-low; cook, uncovered, 8 to 10 minutes or until chicken is cooked through (170°F). Drain and let stand until cool enough to handle.

Italian Three-Cheese Macaroni

2	cups uncooked elbow macaroni
¼	cup (½ stick) butter
3	tablespoons all-purpose flour
1	teaspoon Italian seasoning
½	teaspoon salt
½	teaspoon black pepper
2	cups milk
¾	cup (3 ounces) shredded Cheddar cheese
¼	cup grated Parmesan cheese
1	can (about 14 ounces) diced tomatoes, drained
1	cup (4 ounces) shredded mozzarella cheese
½	cup dry bread crumbs

1. Preheat oven to 350°F. Spray 2-quart baking dish with nonstick cooking spray.

2. Cook macaroni according to package directions until al dente. Drain and return to saucepan; keep warm.

3. Melt butter in medium saucepan over medium heat. Whisk in flour, Italian seasoning, salt and pepper until smooth. Gradually whisk in milk; cook until slightly thickened, whisking frequently. Add Cheddar cheese and Parmesan cheese; stir until smooth.

4. Layer half of pasta, half of tomatoes and half of cheese sauce in prepared dish. Repeat layers. Sprinkle mozzarella and bread crumbs evenly over casserole.

5. Cover and bake 30 minutes or until heated through. Uncover and bake 5 minutes or until top is golden brown.

Makes 4 servings

Mediterranean Mac and Cheese

8	ounces uncooked elbow macaroni or other small pasta shape
1	tablespoon olive oil
1	red bell pepper, cut into slivers
1	bunch (about ¾ pound) asparagus, cut into bite-size pieces
¼	cup (½ stick) butter, divided
¼	cup all-purpose flour
1¾	cups warm milk
1	teaspoon minced fresh thyme
	Salt and black pepper
1	cup (4 ounces) shredded mozzarella cheese
1	cup bite-size pieces cooked chicken
4	ounces garlic and herb flavored goat cheese, crumbled
¼	cup plain dry bread crumbs

1. Preheat oven to 350°F. Cook macaroni according to package directions until almost al dente. Rinse under cold running water to stop cooking; drain.

2. Meanwhile, heat oil in medium skillet over medium-high heat. Add bell pepper; cook and stir 3 minutes. Add asparagus; cook and stir 3 minutes or until crisp-tender. Remove from skillet.

3. Melt 3 tablespoons butter over medium heat in large saucepan or deep skillet until bubbly. Whisk in flour until smooth; cook and stir 2 minutes without browning. Gradually whisk in milk; cook 6 to 8 minutes until mixture begins to bubble and thickens slightly, whisking frequently. Add thyme and season with salt and black pepper. Remove from heat. Stir in mozzarella cheese until melted.

4. Stir pasta, bell pepper, asparagus and chicken into cheese sauce; fold in goat cheese. Transfer to 2-quart baking dish. Top with bread crumbs and dot with remaining 1 tablespoon butter.

5. Bake 25 to 30 minutes or until lightly browned and bubbly.

Makes 4 to 6 servings

Mac and Cheesiest

8	ounces uncooked elbow macaroni
¼	cup (½ stick) butter
5	tablespoons all-purpose flour
1	teaspoon salt
¼	teaspoon ground nutmeg
¼	teaspoon ground black pepper
2¾	cups warm milk
2	to 3 drops hot pepper sauce (optional)
2	cups (8 ounces) shredded Cheddar cheese, divided
¾	cup (3 ounces) shredded aged Gouda cheese
½	cup (2 ounces) shredded American cheese
½	cup (2 ounces) shredded Gruyère or Swiss cheese

1. Preheat oven to 350°F. Cook pasta according to package directions until barely al dente. Drain; rinse under cold running water to stop cooking.

2. Melt butter in large saucepan or deep skillet over medium heat until bubbly. Whisk in flour, salt, nutmeg and black pepper until smooth; cook and stir 2 minutes without browning. Gradually whisk in milk; cook 6 to 8 minutes, whisking frequently until mixture begins to bubble and thickens slightly. Add hot pepper sauce, if desired. Remove from heat. Stir in 1½ cups Cheddar cheese, Gouda cheese, American cheese and Gruyère cheese until smooth.

3. Stir pasta into cheese sauce. Transfer to 2-quart baking dish; sprinkle with remaining ½ cup Cheddar cheese.

4. Bake 20 to 30 minutes or until golden brown.

Makes 6 servings

Baked Pasta and Cheese Supreme

   8   ounces uncooked fusilli pasta or other corkscrew-shaped pasta
  12   slices bacon, diced
   ½   medium onion, chopped
   2   cloves garlic, minced
   2   teaspoons dried oregano, divided
   1   can (8 ounces) tomato sauce
   1   teaspoon hot pepper sauce (optional)
  1½   cups (6 ounces) shredded Cheddar or Colby cheese
   ½   cup fresh bread crumbs (from 1 slice of white bread)
   1   tablespoon butter, melted

1. Preheat oven to 400°F. Cook pasta according to package directions until al dente. Drain and return to saucepan; keep warm.

2. Meanwhile, cook bacon in large cast iron or ovenproof skillet over medium heat until crisp. Drain on paper towels; set aside.

3. Add onion, garlic and 1 teaspoon oregano to skillet; cook and stir 3 minutes or until onion is translucent. Stir in tomato sauce and hot pepper sauce, if desired. Add pasta and cheese; stir to coat.

4. Combine bacon, bread crumbs, remaining 1 teaspoon oregano and butter in small bowl; sprinkle over pasta mixture. Bake 10 to 15 minutes or until hot and bubbly.

Makes 4 servings

Cheesy Spinach Bake

8 ounces uncooked fresh spinach fettuccine noodles
1 tablespoon vegetable oil
1½ cups fresh mushroom slices
2 green onions, finely chopped
1 teaspoon minced garlic
1 package (10 ounces) frozen spinach, thawed and drained
2 tablespoons water
1 container (15 ounces) ricotta cheese
¾ cup whipping cream
1 egg
½ teaspoon salt
½ teaspoon ground nutmeg
¼ teaspoon black pepper
½ cup (2 ounces) shredded Swiss cheese

1. Preheat oven to 350°F. Spray 1½-quart baking dish with nonstick cooking spray. Cook pasta according to package directions until barely tender. Drain and return to saucepan; keep warm.

2. Heat oil in medium skillet over medium heat. Add mushrooms, green onions and garlic; cook and stir until mushrooms are softened. Add spinach and water; cover and cook about 3 minutes or until spinach is wilted.

3. Combine ricotta cheese, cream, egg, salt, nutmeg and black pepper in large bowl. Gently stir in noodles and vegetables until well blended. Spread in prepared baking dish. Sprinkle with Swiss cheese.

4. Bake 25 to 30 minutes or until knife inserted halfway into center comes out clean.

Makes 4 to 6 servings

quick & cheesy

Cheddar and Cavatappi

8 ounces uncooked whole wheat cavatappi pasta (about 3 cups)

6 tablespoons butter, divided

3 shallots, thinly sliced

5 tablespoons all-purpose flour

½ teaspoon salt

½ teaspoon dry mustard

1 cup milk

1 cup whipping cream

2 drops hot pepper sauce (optional)

3 cups (12 ounces) shredded Cheddar cheese

1 cup peas

¼ cup plain dry bread crumbs

1. Preheat oven to 350°F. Cook pasta according to package directions until barely al dente. Drain; rinse under cold running water to stop cooking.

2. Meanwhile, melt 1 tablespoon butter in medium skillet over low heat. Add shallots; cook and stir 5 to 7 minutes or until well browned. Remove from heat.

3. Melt 4 tablespoons butter in large saucepan or deep skillet over medium heat until bubbly. Whisk in flour, salt and mustard until smooth; cook and stir 2 minutes without browning. Gradually whisk in milk and cream; cook 4 to 6 minutes until mixture begins to bubble and thicken, whisking frequently. Stir in hot pepper sauce, if desired.

4. Reduce heat to low; gradually stir in Cheddar cheese until smooth. Add pasta, shallots and peas. Spread in 1½-quart baking dish; sprinkle with bread crumbs.

5. Bake 20 to 25 minutes or until hot and bubbly.

Shells and Fontina

8	ounces uncooked small whole wheat pasta shells
1¾	cups milk
4	large fresh sage leaves (optional)
3	tablespoons butter
4	tablespoons all-purpose flour
½	cup tomato sauce
	Salt and black pepper
¾	cup grated Parmesan cheese, divided
5½	ounces fontina cheese, shredded*
¼	cup plain dry bread crumbs

It is easier to shred fontina cheese if it is very cold. Keep it in the refrigerator or place it in the freezer for 10 minutes before shredding.

1. Preheat oven to 350°F. Cook pasta according to package directions until barely al dente. Drain; rinse under cold running water to stop cooking.

2. Meanwhile, heat milk with sage leaves, if desired, in small saucepan over medium heat; do not boil. Melt butter in large saucepan over medium heat until bubbly. Whisk in flour until smooth; cook and stir 2 minutes without browning. Remove sage and gradually whisk in milk; cook 4 to 5 minutes until mixture begins to bubble and thickens slightly, whisking frequently. Stir in tomato sauce and season with salt and pepper. Remove from heat; stir in ½ cup Parmesan cheese until smooth.

3. Add pasta to sauce; stir to coat. Spoon one third of pasta mixture into 2-quart baking dish. Top with one third of shredded fontina cheese. Repeat layers twice. Sprinkle with bread crumbs and remaining ¼ cup Parmesan.

4. Bake 20 to 25 minutes or until hot and bubbly.

Makes 4 to 6 servings

Reuben Noodle Bake

8   ounces uncooked egg noodles

5   ounces thinly sliced deli-style corned beef

2   cups (8 ounces) shredded Swiss cheese

1   can (about 14 ounces) sauerkraut with caraway seeds, drained

½   cup Thousand Island dressing

½   cup milk

1   tablespoon prepared mustard

2   slices pumpernickel bread

1   tablespoon butter, melted

1. Preheat oven to 350°F. Spray 13×9-inch baking dish with nonstick cooking spray. Cook noodles according to package directions until al dente. Drain and return to saucepan; keep warm.

2. Meanwhile, cut corned beef into bite-size pieces. Combine noodles, corned beef, cheese and sauerkraut in large bowl. Transfer to prepared baking dish.

3. Combine dressing, milk and mustard in small bowl. Spoon evenly over noodle mixture.

4. Tear bread into large pieces; process in food processor or blender until crumbs form. Add butter; pulse to combine. Sprinkle over casserole.

5. Bake 25 to 30 minutes or until heated through.

Makes 6 servings

No Boiling Mexicali Mac & Cheese Bake

    1   jar (1 pound) RAGÚ® Cheesy! Double Cheddar Sauce
    1½ cups water
    1   can (4 ounces) diced green chilies, undrained
    1   cup chopped fresh tomatoes
    1   cup (about 4 ounces) shredded Monterey Jack cheese, divided
    8   ounces uncooked elbow macaroni

1. Preheat oven to 400°F.

2. In large bowl, combine Double Cheddar Sauce, water, chilies, tomatoes and ½ cup cheese. Stir in uncooked macaroni.

3. In 2-quart casserole, spoon macaroni mixture, then cover tightly with aluminum foil. Bake 45 minutes. Remove foil and sprinkle with remaining ½ cup cheese. Bake, uncovered, an additional 5 minutes. Let stand 5 minutes before serving.

Makes 8 servings

Prep Time: 5 minutes
Cook Time: 50 minutes

Easy Pumpkin-Pasta Bake

Nonstick cooking spray
1   box (14.5 ounces) whole wheat penne or other short-cut pasta, prepared according to package directions
1   pound (about 4 links) sweet or spicy lean Italian turkey sausage, casings removed
1   tablespoon finely chopped garlic
1   jar (24 to 26 ounces) marinara sauce
½   cup water or dry red or white wine
1   can (15 ounces) LIBBY'S® 100% Pure Pumpkin
4   tablespoons (0.75 ounce) shredded Parmesan cheese, *divided*
1   cup (4 ounces) shredded low-moisture part-skim mozzarella cheese

PREHEAT oven to 375°F. Spray 3-quart casserole dish or 13×9-inch baking dish with nonstick cooking spray.

COOK sausage in large skillet over medium-high heat until cooked through. Stir in garlic; cook for 1 minute. Stir in marinara sauce (reserve jar). Add water or wine to jar; cover and shake. Pour into skillet along with pumpkin and *2 tablespoons* Parmesan cheese. Stir well. Stir in prepared pasta. Spoon into prepared dish. Sprinkle with *remaining 2 tablespoons* Parmesan cheese and mozzarella cheese; cover.

BAKE for 15 minutes. Carefully remove cover; bake for an additional 5 minutes or until cheese is melted and bubbly.

Makes 10 servings

Prep Time: 15 minutes
Cooking Time: 25 minutes

quick & cheesy

Old-Fashioned Macaroni and Cheese with Broccoli

2	cups (8 ounces) uncooked elbow macaroni
3	cups small broccoli florets
2	tablespoons butter
2	tablespoons all-purpose flour
½	teaspoon salt
⅛	teaspoon black pepper
1¾	cups milk
1½	cups (6 ounces) shredded sharp Cheddar cheese

1. Cook pasta according to package directions until tender, adding broccoli during last 5 minutes of cooking time. Drain and return to saucepan; keep warm.

2. Meanwhile, melt butter in small saucepan over medium heat. Whisk in flour, salt and pepper until smooth; cook and stir 1 minute without browning. Gradually whisk in milk; bring to a boil over medium-high heat, stirring frequently. Reduce heat and simmer 2 minutes. Remove from heat. Gradually stir in cheese until melted.

3. Add sauce to pasta and broccoli; stir until blended.

Makes 4 to 6 servings

sides & salads

Pesto Panzanella

1	package (10 ounces) refrigerated tortellini, cooked and drained
½	cup olive oil
½	cup red wine vinegar
1	tablespoon pesto sauce
3	cups toasted bread cubes
1	cup mozzarella cheese cubes
½	cup sliced pepperoni
⅓	cup pitted kalamata olives, sliced
¼	cup thinly sliced red onion

1. Cook tortellini according to package directions; drain.

2. Whisk oil, vinegar and pesto in large bowl. Add bread cubes, tortellini, cheese, pepperoni, olives and onion; toss to coat.

3. Refrigerate at least 1 hour before serving.

Makes 4 to 6 servings

Lentil and Orzo Pasta Salad

8	cups water
½	cup dried lentils, rinsed and sorted
4	ounces uncooked orzo
1½	cups quartered cherry tomatoes
¾	cup finely chopped celery
½	cup chopped red onion
2	ounces pitted olives (about 16 olives), coarsely chopped
3	to 4 tablespoons cider vinegar
1	tablespoon dried basil
1	tablespoon olive oil
1	clove garlic, minced
⅛	teaspoon red pepper flakes
4	ounces feta cheese with sun-dried tomatoes and basil

1. Bring water to boil in Dutch oven over high heat. Add lentils; cook 12 minutes.

2. Add orzo; cook 10 minutes or just until tender. Drain; rinse under cold water to cool completely.

3. Meanwhile, combine tomatoes, celery, onion, olives, vinegar, basil, oil, garlic and red pepper flakes in large bowl. Add lentil mixture; toss gently to blend. Add cheese; toss gently. Let stand 15 minutes before serving.

Makes 4 servings

Gremolata Pasta Skillet

- 2 **tablespoons olive oil**
- 3 **cloves garlic, minced**
- 2 **cups chicken broth**
- 1 **package (9 ounces) grilled chicken breast strips**
- 2 **tablespoons lemon juice**
- 2 **cups uncooked farfalle (bowtie) pasta**
- ¼ **cup chopped fresh parsley**
- ¼ **cup shredded Parmesan cheese, plus additional for serving**
- 1 **tablespoon grated lemon peel**
  Freshly ground black pepper

1. Heat oil in large nonstick skillet over medium heat. Add garlic; cook 2 to 3 minutes or until soft. Add broth, chicken and lemon juice; bring to a boil.

2. Stir in pasta. Reduce heat to medium-low; cover and cook 10 minutes or until pasta is tender.

3. Stir in parsley, ¼ cup Parmesan cheese and lemon peel. Sprinkle with black pepper and additional cheese, if desired.

Makes 4 servings

Green Bean, Walnut and Blue Cheese Pasta Salad

2   cups uncooked gemelli pasta
2   cups trimmed halved green beans
3   tablespoons olive oil
2   tablespoons white wine vinegar
1   tablespoon chopped fresh thyme *or* 1 teaspoon dried thyme
1   tablespoon Dijon mustard
1   tablespoon fresh lemon juice
1   teaspoon honey
¼   teaspoon salt
¼   teaspoon black pepper
½   cup chopped walnuts, toasted*
½   cup crumbled blue cheese

To toast walnuts, spread in single layer in heavy-bottomed skillet. Cook over medium heat 1 to 2 minutes until nuts are lightly browned, stirring frequently. Remove from skillet immediately. Cool before using.

1. Cook pasta according to package directions until tender, adding green beans during last 4 minutes of cooking. Drain. Transfer to large bowl.

2. Meanwhile, whisk oil, vinegar, thyme, mustard, lemon juice, honey, salt and pepper in medium bowl until smooth and well blended.

3. Pour dressing over pasta and green beans; toss to coat evenly. Stir in walnuts and cheese. Serve warm or cover and refrigerate until ready to serve.**

If serving cold, stir walnuts into salad just before serving.

Makes 8 servings

Spinach, Chicken & Penne Toss

1   package (5 ounces) DOLE® Baby Spinach with Tender Reds, Baby Arugula with Baby Spinach or other DOLE® Salad variety

2   cups cooked penne pasta

1½   cups shredded cooked deli-roasted chicken or deli-sliced chicken or turkey, cut into bite-size strips

⅔   cup slivered drained oil-packed sun-dried tomatoes

⅓   cup toasted pine nuts or slivered almonds

½   cup shredded Parmesan cheese

½   cup bottled red wine vinaigrette or balsamic vinegar dressing

• Place salad blend and all remaining ingredients except dressing in a large salad bowl.

• Toss ingredients well with salad dressing; serve immediately.

Makes 4 servings

Prep Time: 15 minutes

Fettuccine Niçoise Salad

8   ounces green beans, cut into 2-inch pieces
1   package (9 ounces) fresh fettuccine
½   cup coarsely chopped pitted niçoise or kalamata olives
2   tomatoes, cored and chopped
1   can (6 ounces) tuna packed in water, drained and flaked
¼   cup olive oil
1   tablespoon white wine vinegar or fresh lemon juice
¼   teaspoon salt
¼   teaspoon black pepper
¼   cup finely chopped fresh basil

1. Bring large saucepan of salted water to a boil. Add green beans; cook 2 to 5 minutes or until bright green and crisp-tender. Remove beans from water using slotted spoon; drain well.

2. Return water to a boil. Add fettuccine; cook according to package directions until tender. Drain well. Arrange fettuccine, green beans, olives, tomatoes and tuna on plates.

3. Whisk oil, vinegar, salt and pepper in small bowl; pour over salad. Sprinkle with basil.

Makes 4 servings

Skillet Pesto Tortellini

1¼   **cups water**
1¼   **cups milk**
  1   **package (about 1 ounce) creamy pesto sauce mix**
  1   **package (16 ounces) frozen vegetable medley**
  1   **package (12 ounces) frozen tortellini**
      Dash ground red pepper
  ½   **cup (2 ounces) shredded mozzarella cheese**

1. Combine water, milk and sauce mix in large deep skillet. Bring to a boil over high heat. Stir in vegetables, tortellini and ground red pepper; return to a boil.

2. Reduce heat to medium-high. Cook, uncovered, 8 to 10 minutes or until tortellini are tender and sauce has thickened, stirring occasionally.

3. Sprinkle with mozzarella cheese just before serving.

Makes 4 servings

Sweet and Sour Broccoli Pasta Salad

8 ounces uncooked corkscrew pasta (cellentani)

2 cups broccoli florets

⅔ cup shredded carrots

1 medium Red or Golden Delicious apple, cored, seeded and chopped

⅓ cup plain yogurt

⅓ cup apple juice

3 tablespoons cider vinegar

1 tablespoon olive oil

1 tablespoon Dijon mustard

1 teaspoon honey

½ teaspoon dried thyme

Lettuce leaves (optional)

1. Cook pasta according to package directions until tender, adding broccoli during last 2 minutes of cooking. Drain; rinse under cold running water to cool completely. Transfer to large bowl; stir in carrots and apple.

2. Whisk yogurt, apple juice, vinegar, oil, mustard, honey and thyme in medium bowl until smooth and well blended. Pour over pasta mixture; toss to coat.

3. Serve pasta salad on lettuce-lined plates, if desired.

Makes 6 servings

Warm Chicken and Couscous Salad

12 ounces chicken tenders or boneless skinless chicken breasts, cut into strips

2 teaspoons Cajun or blackened seasoning

1 tablespoon olive oil

1 teaspoon minced garlic

2 cups frozen broccoli, carrot and red bell pepper blend

1 can (about 14 ounces) chicken broth

1 cup uncooked couscous

3 cups packed torn spinach leaves

¼ cup poppy seed dressing

1. Toss chicken with Cajun seasoning in medium bowl. Heat oil in large nonstick skillet over medium-high heat. Add chicken mixture and garlic; cook and stir 3 minutes or until chicken is cooked through.

2. Add vegetables and broth to skillet; bring to a boil. Stir in couscous. Remove from heat. Cover and let stand 5 minutes. Stir in spinach; transfer to serving plates. Drizzle with dressing.

Makes 4 servings

Classic Italian Pasta Salad

8	ounces rotelle or spiral pasta, cooked and drained
2½	cups assorted cut-up fresh vegetables (broccoli, carrots, tomatoes, bell peppers and onions)
½	cup cubed Cheddar or mozzarella cheese
⅓	cup sliced pitted ripe olives (optional)
1	cup WISH-BONE® Italian Dressing

Combine all ingredients except WISH-BONE® Italian Dressing in large bowl. Add Dressing; toss well. Serve chilled or at room temperature.

Makes 8 side-dish servings

Tip: If preparing a day ahead, refrigerate, then stir in ¼ cup additional WISH-BONE® Dressing before serving.

Variation: For a Creamy Italian Pasta Salad, substitute ½ cup HELLMANN'S® or BEST FOODS® Real Mayonnaise for ½ cup WISH-BONE® Italian Dressing.

Substitution: Also terrific with WISH-BONE® Robusto Italian, Fat Free! Italian, House Italian, Ranch, Light Ranch, Fat-Free! Ranch, Creamy Caesar, Red Wine Vinaigrette or Fat Free! Red Wine Vinaigrette Dressings.

Prep Time: 20 minutes

sides & salads

Pasta-Salmon Salad

8	ounces uncooked rotini pasta
1	can (7 ounces) salmon, drained, bones removed and flaked
1	cup sliced celery
½	cup chopped green onions
⅔	cup mayonnaise
1	tablespoon Dijon mustard
¼	teaspoon salt
⅛	teaspoon black pepper

1. Cook pasta according to package directions until tender. Drain; rinse under cold water to cool completely. Transfer to large bowl; stir in salmon, celery and green onions.

2. Whisk mayonnaise, mustard, salt and pepper in small bowl; mix well. Add to pasta mixture; stir until well blended.

Makes 4 servings

Chickpea Pasta Salad

  4 ounces uncooked spinach rotini or fusilli pasta
  1 can (about 15 ounces) chickpeas, drained and rinsed
  ½ cup chopped red bell pepper
  ⅓ cup chopped celery
  ⅓ cup finely chopped carrot
  2 green onions, chopped
  3 tablespoons balsamic vinegar
  2 tablespoons mayonnaise
  2 teaspoons whole grain mustard
  ½ teaspoon black pepper
  ¼ teaspoon dried Italian seasoning
     Lettuce and cherry tomatoes (optional)

1. Cook pasta according to package directions until tender. Drain; rinse under cold water to cool completely. Transfer to large bowl; stir in chickpeas, bell pepper, celery, carrot and green onions.

2. Whisk vinegar, mayonnaise, mustard, black pepper and Italian seasoning in small bowl until blended. Pour over salad; toss to coat. Cover and refrigerate up to 8 hours.

3. Serve pasta salad on lettuce-lined plates with cherry tomatoes, if desired.

Makes 6 to 8 servings

Cold Peanut Noodle and Edamame Salad

½ (8-ounce) package brown rice pad thai noodles*
3 tablespoons soy sauce
2 tablespoons toasted sesame oil
2 tablespoons unseasoned rice vinegar
1 tablespoon sugar
1 tablespoon finely grated fresh ginger
1 tablespoon creamy peanut butter
1 tablespoon sriracha or hot chili sauce
2 teaspoons minced garlic
½ cup thawed frozen shelled edamame
¼ cup shredded carrots
¼ cup sliced green onions
Chopped peanuts

Brown rice pad thai noodles can be found in the Asian section of the supermarket. Four ounces whole wheat spaghetti may be substituted, if desired.

1. Prepare noodles according to package directions for pasta. Drain; rinse under cold water to cool completely. Cut noodles into 3-inch lengths. Place in large bowl.

2. Whisk soy sauce, oil, vinegar, sugar, ginger, peanut butter, sriracha and garlic in small bowl until smooth and well blended.

3. Gently toss noodles with dressing. Stir in edamame and carrots. Cover and refrigerate at least 30 minutes to allow flavors to blend.

4. Top with green onions and peanuts just before serving.

Makes 4 servings

sides & salads

Pasta and Potatoes with Pesto

3 medium red potatoes, cut into chunks
8 ounces uncooked linguine
¾ cup peas
1 container (about 7 ounces) pesto sauce
¼ cup plus 2 tablespoons grated Parmesan cheese, divided
¼ teaspoon salt
¼ teaspoon black pepper

1. Place potatoes in medium saucepan; cover with water. Bring to a boil over high heat. Reduce heat; cook, uncovered, 10 minutes or until potatoes are tender. Drain and return to saucepan; keep warm.

2. Meanwhile, cook linguine according to package directions until tender, adding peas during last 3 minutes of cooking. Drain and return to saucepan. Add potatoes, pesto sauce, ¼ cup Parmesan cheese, salt and pepper; gently stir to coat.

3. Sprinkle with remaining 2 tablespoons Parmesan cheese just before serving.

Makes 6 servings

suppertime soups

Souped-Up Soup

2 cans (10 ounces each) condensed tomato soup, plus 3 cans water
2 carrots, peeled and sliced
½ cup uncooked elbow macaroni
½ cup chopped celery
½ cup diced zucchini
1 teaspoon dried Italian seasoning
1 cup croutons
¼ cup grated Parmesan cheese

1. Combine soup and water in medium saucepan over medium heat. Add carrots, macaroni, celery, zucchini and Italian seasoning. Bring to a boil. Reduce heat; simmer 10 minutes or until macaroni and vegetables are tender.

2. Top with croutons and Parmesan cheese just before serving.

Makes 4 servings

Beef and Pasta Soup

1	tablespoon vegetable oil
8	ounces boneless beef round steak, cut into ½-inch cubes
1	medium onion, chopped
3	cloves garlic, minced
4	cups beef broth
1	can (10¾ ounces) tomato purée
2	teaspoons dried Italian seasoning
2	whole bay leaves
1	package (9 ounces) frozen Italian green beans
½	cup uncooked orzo or rosamarina pasta
	Salt and black pepper
	Grated Parmesan cheese

1. Heat oil in Dutch oven or large saucepan over medium-high heat. Add beef, onion and garlic; cook and stir until meat is browned on all sides and onion is slightly tender.

2. Stir in broth, tomato purée, Italian seasoning and bay leaves. Bring to a boil over high heat. Reduce heat to medium-low; simmer, uncovered, 45 minutes.

3. Add green beans and pasta. Bring to a boil over high heat. Reduce heat to medium; simmer, uncovered, 8 minutes or until beans and pasta are tender, stirring frequently. Season with salt and pepper.

4. Remove and discard bay leaves. Serve with Parmesan cheese.

Makes 4 to 6 servings

Thai Noodle Soup

1	package (3 ounces) ramen noodles, any flavor*
12	ounces chicken tenders
2	cans (about 14 ounces each) chicken broth
¼	cup shredded carrots
¼	cup frozen snow peas
2	tablespoons thinly sliced green onion
½	teaspoon minced garlic
¼	teaspoon ground ginger
3	tablespoons chopped fresh cilantro
½	lime, cut into 4 wedges

Discard seasoning packet.

1. Break noodles into pieces. Cook noodles according to package directions until tender. Drain and return to saucepan; keep warm.

2. Cut chicken into ½-inch pieces. Combine broth and chicken in large saucepan or Dutch oven; bring to a boil over medium heat. Cook 2 minutes.

3. Add carrots, snow peas, green onion, garlic and ginger. Reduce heat to low; simmer 3 minutes. Add noodles and cilantro; heat through. Serve with lime wedges.

Makes 4 servings

Pesto Tortellini Soup

  1   **package (9 ounces) refrigerated cheese tortellini**
  3   **cans (about 14 ounces each) vegetable broth**
  1   **jar (7 ounces) roasted red peppers, drained and thinly sliced**
 ¾   **cup peas**
  3   **to 4 cups packed stemmed fresh spinach**
  1   **to 2 tablespoons pesto sauce**
      Grated Parmesan cheese (optional)

1. Cook tortellini according to package directions; drain.

2. Meanwhile, bring broth to a boil in large saucepan or Dutch oven over high heat. Add tortellini, roasted peppers and peas; return to a boil. Reduce heat to medium; simmer 1 minute.

3. Remove from heat; stir in spinach and pesto. Garnish with Parmesan cheese.

Makes 6 servings

Note: To easily remove stems from spinach leaves, fold each leaf in half, then pull stem toward top of leaf. Discard stems.

Minestrone Soup

¾ cup uncooked small shell pasta

2 cans (about 14 ounces each) vegetable broth

1 can (28 ounces) crushed tomatoes in tomato purée

1 can (about 15 ounces) white beans, rinsed and drained

1 package (16 ounces) frozen vegetable medley, such as broccoli, green beans, carrots and red peppers

4 to 6 teaspoons pesto sauce

1. Cook pasta according to package directions until tender. Drain and return to saucepan; keep warm.

2. Meanwhile, combine broth, tomatoes and beans in large saucepan. Cover and bring to a boil over high heat. Reduce heat to low; simmer 3 to 5 minutes.

3. Stir in vegetables; return to a boil over high heat. Stir in pasta. Reduce heat to medium-low; simmer until heated through.

4. Ladle soup into bowls; top each serving with 1 teaspoon pesto.

Makes 4 to 6 servings

suppertime soups

Quick and Zesty Vegetable Soup

1   lb. lean ground beef
½   cup chopped onion
    Salt and pepper
2   cans (14.5 oz. each) DEL MONTE® Italian Recipe Stewed
        Tomatoes
2   cans (14 oz. each) beef broth
1   can (14.5 oz.) DEL MONTE® Mixed Vegetables
½   cup uncooked medium egg noodles
½   tsp. dried oregano

1. Brown meat with onion in large saucepan. Cook until onion is tender; drain. Season to taste with salt and pepper.

2. Stir in remaining ingredients. Bring to boil; reduce heat.

3. Cover and simmer 15 minutes or until noodles are tender.

Makes 8 servings

Prep Time: 5 minutes
Cook Time: 15 minutes

suppertime soups

Fresh Tomato Pasta Soup

1	tablespoon olive oil
½	cup chopped onion
1	clove garlic, minced
3	pounds fresh tomatoes (about 9 medium), coarsely chopped
3	cups vegetable broth
1	tablespoon minced fresh basil
1	tablespoon minced fresh marjoram
1	tablespoon minced fresh oregano
1	teaspoon whole fennel seeds
½	teaspoon black pepper
¾	cup uncooked orzo, rosamarina or other small pasta
½	cup (2 ounces) shredded mozzarella cheese

1. Heat oil in large saucepan over medium heat. Add onion and garlic; cook and stir about 5 minutes or until onion is tender.

2. Add tomatoes, broth, basil, marjoram, oregano, fennel seeds and pepper; bring to a boil. Reduce heat to low; cover and simmer 25 minutes. Remove from heat; cool slightly.

3. Purée tomato mixture in batches in food processor or blender. Return to saucepan; bring to a boil. Add pasta; cook 7 to 9 minutes or until tender.

4. Sprinkle with mozzarella cheese just before serving.

Makes 8 servings

Asian Chicken Noodle Soup

3½	cups SWANSON® Chicken Broth (Regular, Natural Goodness® **or** Certified Organic)
1	teaspoon soy sauce
1	teaspoon ground ginger
	Generous dash ground black pepper
1	medium carrot, diagonally sliced
1	stalk celery, diagonally sliced
½	red pepper, cut into 2-inch-long strips
2	green onions, diagonally sliced
1	clove garlic, minced
½	cup broken-up **uncooked** curly Asian noodles
1	cup shredded cooked chicken

1. Heat the broth, soy sauce, ginger, black pepper, carrot, celery, red pepper, green onions and garlic in a 2-quart saucepan over medium-high heat to a boil.

2. Stir the noodles and chicken in the saucepan. Reduce the heat to medium and cook for 10 minutes or until the noodles are done.

Makes 4 servings

Kitchen Tip: For an Interesting Twist: Use **1 cup** sliced bok choy for the celery and **2 ounces uncooked** cellophane noodles for the curly Asian noodles. Reduce the cook time to 5 minutes.

Prep Time: 5 minutes
Cook Time: 20 minutes
Total Time: 25 minutes

Pizza Meatball and Noodle Soup

1 can (about 14 ounces) beef broth
½ cup chopped onion
½ cup chopped carrot
2 ounces uncooked whole wheat spaghetti, broken into 2-inch pieces
1 cup zucchini slices, cut in half
8 ounces frozen fully cooked Italian-style meatballs, thawed
1 can (8 ounces) tomato sauce
½ cup (2 ounces) shredded mozzarella cheese

1. Combine broth, onion, carrot and spaghetti in large saucepan. Bring to a boil over medium-high heat. Reduce heat to low; cover and simmer 3 minutes.

2. Add zucchini, meatballs and tomato sauce; return to a boil. Reduce heat to low; cover and simmer 8 to 9 minutes or until meatballs are heated through and spaghetti is tender, stirring occasionally.

3. Sprinkle with mozzarella cheese just before serving.

Makes 2 to 4 servings

Chicken Tortellini Soup

6   cups chicken broth

1   package (9 ounces) refrigerated cheese and spinach tortellini

1   package (about 6 ounces) refrigerated fully cooked chicken breast strips, cut into bite-size pieces

2   cups baby spinach

4   to 6 tablespoons grated Parmesan cheese

1   tablespoon chopped fresh chives *or* 2 tablespoons sliced green onion

1. Bring broth to a boil in large saucepan over high heat; add tortellini. Reduce heat to medium; cook 5 minutes. Stir in chicken and spinach.

2. Reduce heat to low; cook 3 minutes or until chicken is heated through. Sprinkle with Parmesan cheese and chives just before serving.

Makes 4 servings

Tomato and Pasta Soup

5	cups chicken or vegetable broth
2½	cups uncooked farfalle (bowtie) or rotini pasta
1	tablespoon minced onion
1	teaspoon sugar
1	teaspoon dried Italian seasoning
½	teaspoon minced garlic
¼	teaspoon black pepper
1	can (about 28 ounces) crushed tomatoes
4	to 6 slices bacon, crisp-cooked and crumbled
3	cups chopped fresh spinach
½	cup grated Parmesan cheese

1. Combine broth, pasta, onion, sugar, Italian seasoning, garlic and pepper in large saucepan. Bring to a boil over high heat.

2. Stir in tomatoes and bacon. Reduce heat to medium-low; simmer 10 to 12 minutes or until pasta is tender. Stir in spinach; cook until spinach is wilted.

3. Sprinkle with Parmesan cheese just before serving.

Makes 4 to 5 servings

All-in-One Burger Stew

1   pound ground beef
2   cups frozen Italian-style vegetables
1   can (about 14 ounces) diced tomatoes with basil and garlic
1   can (about 14 ounces) beef broth
2½ cups uncooked medium egg noodles
    Salt and black pepper

1. Brown beef in Dutch oven or large skillet over medium-high heat 6 to 8 minutes, stirring to break up meat. Drain fat.

2. Add vegetables, tomatoes and broth; bring to a boil over high heat.

3. Stir in noodles. Reduce heat to medium; cover and cook 12 to 15 minutes or until vegetables and noodles are tender. Season with salt and pepper.

Makes 6 servings

Pasta Fagioli

1   jar (1 pound 8 ounces) RAGÚ® Chunky Pasta Sauce
1   can (19 ounces) white kidney beans, rinsed and drained
1   package (10 ounces) frozen chopped spinach, thawed
8   ounces ditalini pasta, cooked and drained (reserve 2 cups pasta water)

1. Combine Pasta Sauce, beans, spinach, pasta and reserved pasta water in 6-quart saucepan; heat through.

2. Season, if desired, with salt, ground black pepper and grated Parmesan cheese.

Makes 4 servings

Prep Time: 20 minutes
Cook Time: 10 minutes

weeknight noodles

Creamy Fettuccine with Asparagus and Lima Beans

8   ounces uncooked fettuccine

2   tablespoons butter

2   cups fresh asparagus pieces (about 1 inch long)

1   cup frozen lima beans, thawed

¼   teaspoon black pepper

½   cup vegetable broth

1   cup half-and-half or whipping cream

1   cup grated Parmesan cheese

1. Cook fettuccine according to package directions until tender. Drain and return to saucepan; keep warm.

2. Meanwhile, melt butter in large skillet over medium-high heat. Add asparagus, lima beans and ¼ teaspoon pepper; cook and stir 3 minutes. Add broth; simmer 3 minutes. Add half-and-half; simmer 3 to 4 minutes or until vegetables are tender.

3. Add vegetable mixture and Parmesan cheese to fettuccine; toss well. Serve immediately.

Makes 4 servings

weeknight noodles

Skillet Lasagna with Vegetables

1   tablespoon vegetable oil
8   ounces hot Italian turkey sausage, casings removed
8   ounces ground turkey
2   stalks celery, sliced
⅓   cup chopped onion
2   cups marinara sauce
1⅓   cups water
4   ounces uncooked farfalle (bowtie) pasta
1   medium zucchini, halved lengthwise and cut into ½-inch-thick
     slices
¾   cup chopped green or yellow bell pepper
½   cup ricotta cheese
2   tablespoons grated Parmesan cheese
½   cup (2 ounces) shredded mozzarella cheese

1. Heat oil in large skillet over medium-high heat. Add sausage, turkey, celery and onion; cook and stir until turkey is no longer pink. Stir in marinara sauce and water. Bring to a boil. Stir in pasta. Reduce heat to medium-low; cover and simmer 12 minutes.

2. Stir in zucchini and bell pepper; cover and simmer 2 minutes. Uncover and simmer 4 to 6 minutes or until vegetables are crisp-tender.

3. Combine ricotta cheese and Parmesan cheese in small bowl. Drop by rounded teaspoonfuls on top of mixture in skillet. Sprinkle with mozzarella cheese. Remove from heat; cover and let stand 10 minutes or until mozzarella cheese is melted.

Makes 6 servings

Penne with Broccoli and Sausage

8   ounces uncooked whole wheat penne pasta
8   ounces broccoli florets
8   ounces mild Italian turkey sausage, casings removed
1   medium onion, quartered and sliced
2   cloves garlic, minced
2   teaspoons grated lemon peel
¼   teaspoon salt
⅛   teaspoon black pepper
½   cup shredded Parmesan cheese

1. Cook pasta according to package directions until tender, adding broccoli during last 5 minutes of cooking. Drain and return to saucepan; keep warm.

2. Meanwhile, heat large nonstick skillet over medium heat. Crumble sausage into skillet. Add onion; cook until sausage is browned, stirring to break up meat. Drain fat. Add garlic; cook and stir 1 minute.

3. Add sausage mixture, lemon peel, salt and pepper to pasta mixture; toss until blended. Sprinkle with Parmesan cheese just before serving.

Makes 4 to 6 servings

Skillet Pasta Roma

½   lb. Italian sausage, sliced or crumbled

1   large onion, coarsely chopped

1   large clove garlic, minced

2   cans (14.5 oz. each) DEL MONTE® Diced Tomatoes with Basil, Garlic & Oregano

1   can (8 oz.) DEL MONTE® Tomato Sauce

1   cup water

8   oz. uncooked rotini or other spiral pasta

8   mushrooms, sliced (optional)

    Grated Parmesan cheese and fresh parsley sprigs (optional)

1. Brown sausage in large skillet. Add onion and garlic. Cook until onion is soft; drain. Stir in undrained tomatoes, tomato sauce, water and pasta.

2. Cover and bring to a boil; reduce heat. Simmer, covered, 25 to 30 minutes or until pasta is tender, stirring occasionally.

3. Stir in mushrooms, if desired; simmer 5 minutes. Serve in skillet garnished with cheese and parsley, if desired.

Makes 4 servings

Tuna & Pasta Cheddar Melt

1 can (10½ ounces) CAMPBELL'S® Condensed Chicken Broth
1 soup can water
3 cups **uncooked** corkscrew-shaped pasta (rotini)
1 can (10¾ ounces) CAMPBELL'S® Condensed Cream of
   Mushroom Soup (Regular **or** 98% Fat Free)
1 cup milk
1 can (about 6 ounces) tuna, drained and flaked
1 cup shredded Cheddar cheese (about 4 ounces)
2 tablespoons Italian-seasoned dry bread crumbs
2 teaspoons butter, melted

1. Heat the broth and water in a 12-inch skillet over medium-high heat to a boil. Stir in the pasta. Reduce the heat to medium. Cook until the pasta is tender, stirring often. Do not drain.

2. Stir the soup, milk and tuna in the skillet. Top with the cheese. Stir the bread crumbs and butter in a small bowl. Sprinkle over the tuna mixture. Cook until the cheese is melted.

Makes 4 servings

Serving Suggestion: Serve with steamed whole green beans. For dessert serve clementines.

Prep Time: 10 minutes
Cook Time: 15 minutes
Total Time: 25 minutes

Chicken and Couscous with Pistachios

¾	teaspoon ground allspice
½	teaspoon ground cinnamon
½	teaspoon black pepper
¼	teaspoon ground ginger
¼	teaspoon ground mustard
⅛	teaspoon ground cloves
⅛	teaspoon ground red pepper
⅛	teaspoon ground coriander
12	ounces boneless skinless chicken breasts, cut into 1-inch pieces
½	teaspoon salt
1	tablespoon olive oil
1	can (about 14 ounces) reduced-sodium chicken broth
1	cup uncooked couscous
¼	cup golden raisins
¼	cup shelled pistachio nuts
¼	cup chopped fresh parsley
1	teaspoon grated lemon peel

1. Combine allspice, cinnamon, black pepper, ginger, mustard, cloves, red pepper and coriander in small bowl. Sprinkle chicken with 1 teaspoon of spice mixture and salt.

2. Heat oil in large nonstick skillet over medium-high heat. Add chicken; cook about 3 minutes or until golden and no longer pink in center, turning once.

3. Add broth; bring to a boil. Add couscous and ½ teaspoon spice mixture; cook 1 minute. Stir in raisins, pistachios, parsley and lemon peel; cover and let stand 5 minutes. Fluff with fork before serving.

Makes 4 servings

weeknight noodles

Baked Chicken and Garlic Orzo

1   tablespoon vegetable oil

4   skinless chicken breasts

¼   cup dry white wine

1   can (about 14 ounces) reduced-sodium chicken broth

10   ounces uncooked orzo pasta

1   cup chopped onion

¼   cup water

4   cloves garlic, minced

2   tablespoons chopped fresh parsley

2   teaspoons olive oil

1   teaspoon dried oregano

¼   teaspoon salt

    Paprika

1   teaspoon lemon pepper

1   lemon, cut into 8 wedges (optional)

1. Preheat oven to 350°F. Heat vegetable oil in large cast iron skillet over high heat. Add chicken; cook without turning 1 to 2 minutes or until lightly browned. Remove chicken from skillet; set aside.

2. Reduce heat to medium-high; add wine, stirring to scrape up browned bits from bottom of skillet. Cook 30 seconds or until slightly reduced. Stir in broth, pasta, onion, water, garlic, parsley, olive oil, oregano and salt. Top with chicken. Sprinkle with paprika and lemon pepper.

3. Bake, uncovered, 1 hour 10 minutes or until orzo is tender and chicken is cooked through. Serve with lemon wedges, if desired.

Makes 4 servings

Szechuan Vegetable Lo Mein

2   cans (about 14 ounces each) vegetable broth

2   teaspoons minced garlic

1   teaspoon minced fresh ginger

¼   teaspoon red pepper flakes

1   package (16 ounces) frozen vegetable medley, such as broccoli, carrots, water chestnuts and red bell peppers

2   packages (6 ounces) ramen noodles, any flavor* *or* 5 ounces uncooked angel hair pasta, broken in half

3   tablespoons soy sauce

1   tablespoon dark sesame oil

¼   cup thinly sliced green onions

*Discard seasoning packets.

1. Combine broth, garlic, ginger and red pepper flakes in wok or large skillet. Cover and bring to a boil over high heat. Add vegetables and noodles; cover and return to a boil. Reduce heat to medium-low; simmer, uncovered, 5 to 6 minutes or until vegetables and noodles are tender, stirring occasionally.

2. Stir in soy sauce and sesame oil; cook 3 minutes. Stir in green onions just before serving.

Makes 4 servings

Note: For a heartier dish, add 1 package (14 ounces) extra firm tofu, drained and cut into ¾-inch cubes, or 2 cups chopped cooked chicken in step 2.

Coq au Vin & Pasta

4   large or 8 small chicken thighs (2 to 2½ pounds), trimmed of
      excess fat
2   teaspoons rotisserie or herb chicken seasoning*
1   tablespoon margarine or butter
3   cups (8 ounces) halved or quartered mushrooms
1   medium onion, coarsely chopped
½   cup dry white wine or vermouth
1   package (4.9 ounces) PASTA RONI® Chicken Flavor
½   cup sliced green onions

1 teaspoon paprika and 1 teaspoon garlic salt can be substituted.

1. Sprinkle meaty side of chicken with rotisserie seasoning. In large skillet over medium-high heat, melt margarine. Add chicken, seasoned-side down; cook 3 minutes. Reduce heat to medium-low; turn chicken over.

2. Add mushrooms, onion and wine. Cover; simmer 15 to 18 minutes or until chicken is no longer pink inside. Remove chicken from skillet; set aside.

3. In same skillet, bring 1 cup water to a boil. Stir in pasta, green onions and Special Seasonings. Place chicken over pasta. Reduce heat to medium-low. Cover; gently boil 6 to 8 minutes or until pasta is tender. Let stand 3 to 5 minutes before serving.

Makes 4 servings

Prep Time: 10 minutes
Cook Time: 30 minutes

weeknight noodles

Bolognese Sauce and Penne Pasta

1	pound ground beef
1	cup chopped onion
2	cloves garlic, minced
2	cans (8 ounces each) tomato sauce
½	cup chopped carrots
½	cup water
¼	cup dry red wine
2	teaspoons dried Italian seasoning
2	cups uncooked penne pasta
	Chopped fresh parsley

1. Brown beef, onion and garlic in medium saucepan over medium-high heat 6 to 8 minutes, stirring to break up meat. Drain fat.

2. Add tomato sauce, carrots, water, wine and Italian seasoning; bring to a boil. Reduce heat; simmer 15 minutes.

3. Meanwhile, cook pasta according to package directions until tender; drain. Serve sauce over pasta. Sprinkle with parsley.

Makes 4 servings

Chicken and Linguine in Creamy Tomato Sauce

1	tablespoon olive oil
1	pound boneless, skinless chicken breasts, cut into ½-inch strips
1	jar (1 pound 8 ounces) RAGÚ® Old World Style® Pasta Sauce
2	cups water
8	ounces uncooked linguine or spaghetti
½	cup whipping or heavy cream
1	tablespoon chopped fresh basil leaves *or* ½ teaspoon dried basil leaves, crushed

1. In 12-inch skillet, heat olive oil over medium heat and brown chicken. Remove chicken and set aside.

2. In same skillet, stir in Pasta Sauce and water. Bring to a boil over high heat. Stir in uncooked linguine and return to a boil. Reduce heat to low and simmer covered, stirring occasionally, 15 minutes or until linguine is tender.

3. Stir in cream and basil. Return chicken to skillet and cook 5 minutes or until chicken is thoroughly cooked.

Makes 4 servings

Prep Time: 10 minutes
Cook Time: 30 minutes

Shrimp Caprese Pasta

1	cup uncooked whole wheat penne
2	teaspoons olive oil
2	cups coarsely chopped grape tomatoes
4	tablespoons chopped fresh basil, divided
1	tablespoon balsamic vinegar
2	cloves garlic, minced
¼	teaspoon salt
⅛	teaspoon red pepper flakes
8	ounces medium raw shrimp, peeled and deveined
1	cup grape tomatoes, halved
2	ounces fresh mozzarella pearls

1. Cook pasta according to package directions until tender. Drain, reserving ½ cup cooking water. Return pasta to saucepan and keep warm.

2. Heat oil in large skillet over medium heat. Add chopped tomatoes, reserved ½ cup pasta water, 2 tablespoons basil, vinegar, garlic, salt and red pepper flakes. Cook and stir 10 minutes or until tomatoes begin to soften.

3. Add shrimp and halved tomatoes to skillet; cook and stir 5 minutes or until shrimp turn pink and opaque. Add pasta; cook until heated through.

4. Serve with mozzarella cheese and remaining 2 tablespoons basil.

Makes 4 servings

Apricot Beef with Sesame Noodles

1   beef top sirloin steak (about 1 pound)

3   tablespoons Dijon mustard

3   tablespoons soy sauce

2   packages (3 ounces each) uncooked ramen noodles, any flavor*

2   tablespoons vegetable oil

2   cups (6 ounces) snow peas

1   red bell pepper, diced

¾   cup apricot preserves

½   cup beef broth

3   tablespoons chopped green onions

2   tablespoons toasted sesame seeds,** divided

Discard seasoning packets.

**To toast sesame seeds, spread in small heavy skillet. Cook over medium heat 2 minutes or until golden, stirring frequently.*

1. Cut beef lengthwise in half, then crosswise into ¼-inch strips. Combine beef, mustard and soy sauce in medium resealable food storage bag. Seal bag; turn to coat. Marinate in refrigerator 4 hours or overnight.

2. Cook noodles according to package directions. Drain and return to saucepan; keep warm.

3. Heat oil in wok or large skillet over medium-high heat. Add beef with marinade; stir-fry 2 minutes. Add snow peas and bell pepper; stir-fry 2 minutes. Add noodles, preserves, broth, green onions and 1 tablespoon sesame seeds. Cook 1 minute or until heated through. Top with remaining sesame seeds just before serving.

Makes 4 to 6 servings

one-pot pasta

Polka Dot Lasagna Skillet

1	pound ground turkey or beef
1	package lasagna and sauce meal kit
4	cups hot water
½	cup ricotta cheese
1	egg
3	tablespoons grated Parmesan cheese
2	tablespoons all-purpose flour
2	tablespoons chopped fresh parsley
½	teaspoon dried Italian seasoning
¼	teaspoon black pepper

1. Cook turkey in large skillet over medium-high heat or until no longer pink, stirring to break up meat.

2. Stir in contents of meal kit and hot water; bring to a boil. Reduce heat to low; cover and cook 10 minutes.

3. Meanwhile, stir ricotta, egg, Parmesan, flour, parsley, Italian seasoning and pepper in small bowl until smooth. Drop tablespoonfuls of ricotta mixture over pasta; cover and cook 4 to 5 minutes or until dumplings are set. Remove from heat; let stand 5 minutes before serving.

Makes 4 to 6 servings

one-pot pasta

Stovetop Tuna Casserole

1   **package (12 ounces) deluxe macaroni and cheese dinner with shell pasta**

2   **cups peas**

1   **tablespoon butter**

1   **can (6 ounces) chunk white tuna**

½   **teaspoon black pepper (optional)**

1. Remove cheese sauce pouch from macaroni and cheese; set aside. Bring water to a boil in large saucepan. Stir in pasta. Cook 6 to 8 minutes or until pasta is tender, adding peas during last 3 minutes of cooking. Drain and return to saucepan.

2. Stir in cheese sauce and butter until well blended. Drain tuna and flake with fork. Stir into pasta. Sprinkle with black pepper, if desired.

Makes 4 servings

Tip: Check your fridge for extra veggies to toss into this quick casserole. Stir in ¼ to ½ cup of the extra ingredient with the peas. Try finely chopped carrots, green onions, red onions, mushrooms or celery.

Variation: Preheat oven to 350°F. Spray 8-inch baking dish with nonstick cooking spray. Spread tuna casserole mixture into prepared baking dish. Sprinkle with 1½ cups crushed potato chips or buttery round crackers. Bake 12 to 15 minutes or until topping is lightly browned.

one-pot pasta

Ham and Swiss Penne Skillet

6	ounces uncooked penne pasta
2	slices bread, torn into pieces
5	tablespoons butter, divided
3	tablespoons all-purpose flour
2¾	cups whole milk
1	cup corn
¾	cup peas
6	ounces ham, diced
1	cup (4 ounces) shredded Swiss cheese
½	cup finely chopped green onions
	Salt and black pepper

1. Cook pasta in large saucepan according to package directions until tender. Drain; keep warm.

2. Place bread in food processor; pulse to form coarse crumbs. Melt 2 tablespoons butter in same saucepan over medium heat. Add bread crumbs; cook and stir 2 minutes or until golden. Transfer to plate; set aside.

3. Melt remaining 3 tablespoons butter in same saucepan over medium heat. Whisk in flour until smooth; cook 2 minutes without browning. Gradually whisk in milk; cook 4 minutes or until slightly thickened, whisking frequently.

4. Add pasta, corn, peas, ham, cheese and green onions; stir gently to blend. Season with salt and pepper. Cook 4 minutes or until heated through. Sprinkle with bread crumbs. Serve immediately.

Makes 4 servings

one-pot pasta

Greek Chicken and Pasta Skillet

- 1 tablespoon olive oil
- 1 teaspoon Greek seasoning *or* 1 teaspoon oregano plus dash garlic powder
- ½ teaspoon grated lemon peel
- ½ teaspoon black pepper
- 4 boneless skinless chicken breasts, cut into 1-inch cubes
- 1 can (about 14 ounces) chicken broth
- 1¼ cups uncooked orzo pasta
- 6 ounces pitted green olives, drained
- 4 cloves garlic, minced
- 2 cups packed fresh spinach
- ½ cup crumbled feta cheese

1. Heat oil in large skillet over medium heat. Add seasoning, lemon peel and pepper; cook and stir just until fragrant. Add chicken; cook and stir 4 minutes.

2. Stir in broth, orzo, olives and garlic. Bring to a boil over high heat. Reduce heat; simmer, partially covered, 15 minutes or until pasta is tender and chicken is cooked through, stirring occasionally.

3. Stir in spinach and feta. Cover and let stand 2 to 3 minutes or until spinach wilts.

Makes 4 servings

Chicken with Parmesan Fettuccine

 2   tablespoons butter, divided
 1   pound boneless skinless chicken breasts, cut into bite-size pieces
 1   clove garlic, minced
3½ cups chicken broth
 6   ounces uncooked fettuccine, broken in half
 ½ cup whipping cream
 ½ cup grated Parmesan cheese
 ½ cup finely chopped green onions
 ¼ teaspoon black pepper

1. Melt 1 tablespoon butter in large saucepan over medium heat. Add chicken and garlic; cook and stir 3 minutes or until chicken is cooked through. Transfer to bowl; keep warm.

2. Add broth to saucepan; bring to a boil over high heat. Add pasta; return to a boil. Reduce heat to medium-low; cover and simmer 10 minutes or just until tender. Drain pasta, reserving 2 tablespoons broth. Return pasta to saucepan.

3. Add chicken and cream to pasta. Gradually stir in Parmesan cheese. Stir in green onions, pepper and remaining 1 tablespoon butter; cook 2 minutes or until thickened. Add reserved broth to thin sauce, if necessary.

Makes 4 servings

Farfalle Pasta Bowl

3	cups chicken broth
6	ounces uncooked farfalle (bowtie) pasta
⅛	teaspoon red pepper flakes
1½	cups diced cooked chicken
1	medium tomato, seeded and diced
1	cup packed spring greens or spinach, coarsely chopped
3	tablespoons chopped fresh basil
¼	teaspoon salt
1	cup (4 ounces) shredded mozzarella cheese
4	teaspoons grated Parmesan cheese

1. Bring broth to boil in large saucepan over high heat; add pasta and red pepper flakes. Return to a boil. Reduce heat; cover and simmer 10 minutes or until pasta is al dente.

2. Add chicken; cook 1 minute. Remove from heat; stir in tomato, greens, basil and salt.

3. Top with mozzarella cheese and Parmesan cheese just before serving.

Makes 4 servings

Chicken Florentine in Minutes

3   cups water

1   cup milk

2   tablespoons butter

2   packages (about 4 ounces each) fettuccine Alfredo or stroganoff
     pasta mix

¼   teaspoon black pepper

1   package (about 10 ounces) refrigerated fully cooked chicken
     breast strips, cut into ½-inch pieces

4   cups baby spinach, coarsely chopped

¼   cup diced roasted red pepper

¼   cup sour cream

1. Bring water, milk and butter to a boil in large saucepan over medium-high heat. Stir in pasta mix and black pepper. Reduce heat to medium; cook 8 minutes or until pasta is tender, stirring occasionally.

2. Stir in chicken, spinach and roasted pepper; cook 2 minutes or until heated through. Remove from heat. Stir in sour cream.

Makes 4 servings

Vegetarian Asian Noodles with Peanut Sauce

½ package (about 4 ounces) uncooked udon noodles* *or* 4 ounces uncooked whole wheat spaghetti

1 tablespoon vegetable oil

2 cups snow peas, cut diagonally into bite-size pieces

1 cup shredded carrots

¼ cup chopped green onions

¼ cup hot water

¼ cup peanut butter

2 to 4 tablespoons hot chili sauce with garlic

1 tablespoon soy sauce

¼ cup dry-roasted peanuts

Udon noodles (wheat flour noodles) are usually available in the Asian section of well-stocked supermarkets.

1. Cook noodles in large skillet according to package directions until tender. Drain; keep warm.

2. Heat oil in same skillet over medium-high heat. Add snow peas and carrots; stir-fry 2 minutes. Remove from heat.

3. Add green onions, peanut butter, water, chili sauce and soy sauce to skillet; mix well. Stir in noodles; toss to coat. Sprinkle with peanuts just before serving.

Makes 4 servings

Quick Skillet Chicken & Macaroni Parmesan

1   jar (24 ounces) PREGO® Traditional Italian Sauce **or** Tomato, Basil & Garlic Italian Sauce

¼   cup grated Parmesan cheese

1   can (12.5 ounces) SWANSON® Premium White Chunk Chicken Breast in Water, drained

2   cups elbow pasta, cooked and drained (about 3 cups)

1   cup shredded mozzarella cheese (about 4 ounces)

1. Heat the Italian sauce, Parmesan cheese, chicken and pasta in a 10-inch skillet over medium-high heat to a boil. Reduce the heat to medium and cook for 10 minutes or until the mixture is hot and bubbling, stirring occasionally.

2. Sprinkle with the mozzarella cheese. Let stand for 5 minutes or until the cheese is melted.

Makes 4 servings

Kitchen Tip: You may substitute 3 cans (4.5 ounces **each**) SWANSON® Premium White Chunk Chicken Breast in Water, drained, for the 12.5-ounce can.

Prep Time: 15 minutes
Cook Time: 15 minutes
Stand Time: 5 minutes

one-pot pasta

Shrimp and Pepper Noodle Bowl

2 packages (3 ounces each) shrimp-flavored ramen noodles
8 ounces frozen cooked medium shrimp or frozen cooked baby shrimp
1 cup bell pepper strips
¼ cup chopped green onions
1 tablespoon soy sauce
½ teaspoon hot pepper sauce
2 tablespoons chopped fresh cilantro (optional)

1. Bring 4 cups water to a boil in large saucepan over high heat. Remove seasoning packets from noodles; set aside. Break up noodles; add to water. Add shrimp and bell pepper; cook 3 minutes.

2. Add seasoning packets, green onions, soy sauce and hot pepper sauce; cook 1 minute. Garnish with cilantro.

Makes 4 servings

Country Skillet Supper

1	pound ground beef
1	medium onion, chopped (about ½ cup)
⅛	teaspoon garlic powder
1	can (10¾ ounces) CAMPBELL'S® Condensed Golden Mushroom Soup
1	can (10½ ounces) CAMPBELL'S® Condensed Beef Broth
½	teaspoon dried thyme leaves, crushed
1	can (14.5 ounces) diced tomatoes
1	small zucchini, sliced (about 1 cup)
1½	cups **uncooked** corkscrew-shaped pasta (rotelle)

1. Cook the beef, onion and garlic powder in a 10-inch skillet over medium-high heat until the beef is well browned, stirring frequently to separate meat. Pour off any fat.

2. Stir the soup, broth, thyme, tomatoes and zucchini into the skillet. Heat to a boil. Stir in the pasta and reduce the heat to low. Cook and stir for 15 minutes or until the pasta is tender but still firm.

Makes 4 servings

Prep/Cook Time: 25 minutes

Tempting Tuna Parmesano

1   package (9 ounces) refrigerated fresh angel hair pasta
¼   cup (½ stick) butter
2   cloves garlic, minced
1   cup whipping cream
1   cup peas
¼   teaspoon salt
1   can (6 ounces) white tuna in water, drained
¼   cup grated Parmesan cheese, plus additional for serving
     Salt and black pepper

1. Cook pasta in large skillet according to package directions until al dente (do not overcook). Drain; keep warm.

2. Heat butter and garlic in same skillet over medium-high heat until butter is melted and sizzling. Stir in cream, peas and salt; bring to a boil.

3. Break tuna into chunks and stir into skillet with ¼ cup Parmesan cheese. Add pasta to skillet. Cook until heated through, tossing gently to blend. Season with salt and pepper. Serve with additional Parmesan cheese.

Makes 2 to 3 servings

Easy Skillet Ravioli

1   **package (about 24 ounces) frozen cheese ravioli**
2¼   **cups water**
½   **teaspoon salt**
1   **jar (1 pound 8 ounces) RAGÚ® Chunky Pasta Sauce**
¼   **cup heavy cream, half-and-half, evaporated milk, milk or nondairy creamer (optional)**

1. In 12-inch nonstick skillet, bring ravioli, water and salt to a boil over high heat. Continue boiling, stirring gently to separate ravioli, 5 minutes.

2. Stir in Pasta Sauce. Cook, covered, over medium heat 10 minutes or until ravioli are tender, stirring occasionally. Stir in cream and heat through. Garnish, if desired, with grated Parmesan cheese.

Makes 4 servings

Prep Time: 5 minutes
Cook Time: 20 minutes

Chicken Margherita Alfredo

1	pound boneless, skinless chicken breasts, cut into thin strips
1	tablespoon I CAN'T BELIEVE IT'S NOT BUTTER!® Spread
1½	cups water
½	cup 2% milk
1	package KNORR® PASTA SIDES™–Alfredo Broccoli
1	cup grape tomatoes, halved
¼	cup loosely packed fresh basil leaves, thinly sliced

1. Season chicken, if desired, with salt and black pepper. Melt I CAN'T BELIEVE IT'S NOT BUTTER!® Spread in 12-inch nonstick skillet over medium-high heat and cook chicken, stirring occasionally, until chicken is thoroughly cooked, about 5 minutes. Remove chicken; set aside and keep warm.

2. Stir water and milk into same skillet and bring to a boil over high heat. Stir in KNORR® PASTA SIDES™–Alfredo Broccoli and continue boiling over medium heat, stirring occasionally, 8 minutes or until pasta is tender. Stir in chicken, basil and tomatoes; heat through.

Makes 4 servings

Prep Time: 10 minutes
Cook Time: 15 minutes

Spicy Chicken Chili Mac

1	can (14.5 ounces) whole peeled tomatoes, cut up
2½	cups water
1	cup PACE® Picante Sauce
1	tablespoon chili powder
¼	teaspoon garlic powder **or** 2 cloves garlic, minced
¼	teaspoon salt
¾	cup **uncooked** elbow macaroni
2	cups cubed cooked chicken **or** turkey

1. Mix tomatoes, water, picante sauce, chili powder, garlic and salt in a 10-inch skillet over medium-high heat. Heat to a boil. Stir in the macaroni. Cover and cook over low heat for 15 minutes or until macaroni is done, stirring often.

2. Add the chicken and heat through. Garnish with shredded cheese and sour cream if desired.

Makes 4 servings

Total Time: 25 minutes

Chicken Couscous

1 tablespoon vegetable oil

8 ounces boneless skinless chicken breasts, cut into 1-inch cubes

4 medium zucchini, sliced

1 can (about 14 ounces) diced tomatoes

1 can (about 14 ounces) chicken broth

1 teaspoon dried Italian seasoning

1 cup uncooked whole wheat couscous

1. Heat oil in large skillet over medium-high heat. Add chicken; cook and stir 4 minutes or until lightly browned.

2. Add zucchini, tomatoes, broth and Italian seasoning. Reduce heat to low; simmer 15 minutes, stirring occasionally.

3. Stir in couscous; remove from heat. Cover and let stand 7 minutes. Fluff with fork.

Makes 4 servings

index

index

index

index

acknowledgments

*The publisher would like to thank the companies listed below
for the use of their recipes and photographs in this publication.*

Campbell Soup Company

Del Monte Foods

Dole Food Company, Inc.

The Golden Grain Company®

Nestlé USA

Pinnacle Foods

Unilever

metric conversion chart

VOLUME MEASUREMENTS (dry)

$^1/_8$ teaspoon = 0.5 mL
$^1/_4$ teaspoon = 1 mL
$^1/_2$ teaspoon = 2 mL
$^3/_4$ teaspoon = 4 mL
1 teaspoon = 5 mL
1 tablespoon = 15 mL
2 tablespoons = 30 mL
$^1/_4$ cup = 60 mL
$^1/_3$ cup = 75 mL
$^1/_2$ cup = 125 mL
$^2/_3$ cup = 150 mL
$^3/_4$ cup = 175 mL
1 cup = 250 mL
2 cups = 1 pint = 500 mL
3 cups = 750 mL
4 cups = 1 quart = 1 L

VOLUME MEASUREMENTS (fluid)

1 fluid ounce (2 tablespoons) = 30 mL
4 fluid ounces ($^1/_2$ cup) = 125 mL
8 fluid ounces (1 cup) = 250 mL
12 fluid ounces (1$^1/_2$ cups) = 375 mL
16 fluid ounces (2 cups) = 500 mL

WEIGHTS (mass)

$^1/_2$ ounce = 15 g
1 ounce = 30 g
3 ounces = 90 g
4 ounces = 120 g
8 ounces = 225 g
10 ounces = 285 g
12 ounces = 360 g
16 ounces = 1 pound = 450 g

DIMENSIONS

$^1/_{16}$ inch = 2 mm
$^1/_8$ inch = 3 mm
$^1/_4$ inch = 6 mm
$^1/_2$ inch = 1.5 cm
$^3/_4$ inch = 2 cm
1 inch = 2.5 cm

OVEN TEMPERATURE

250°F = 120°C
275°F = 140°C
300°F = 150°C
325°F = 160°C
350°F = 180°C
375°F = 190°C
400°F = 200°C
425°F = 220°C
450°F = 230°C

BAKING PAN SIZES

Utensil	Size in Inches/Quarts	Metric Volume	Size in Centimeters
Baking or	8×8×2	2 L	20×20×5
Cake Pan	9×9×2	2.5 L	23×23×5
(square or	12×8×2	3 L	30×20×5
rectangular)	13×9×2	3.5 L	33×23×5
Loaf Pan	8×4×3	1.5 L	20×10×7
	9×5×3	2 L	23×13×7
Round Layer	8×1½	1.2 L	20×4
Cake Pan	9×1½	1.5 L	23×4
Pie Plate	8×1¼	750 mL	20×3
	9×1¼	1 L	23×3
Baking Dish	1 quart	1 L	—
or Casserole	1½ quarts	1.5 L	—
	2 quarts	2 L	—